Collateral Damage:
literary biographies

Collateral Damage:
literary biographies

Viginia Aronson

Clare Songbirds
Publishing House

Clare Songbirds Publishing House Poetry Series
ISBN 978-1-957221-34-2
Clare Songbirds Publishing House
Collateral Damage© 2025 Virginia Aronson

Printed in the United States of America
FIRST EDITION

140 Cottage Street
Auburn, New York 13021
www.claresongbirdspub.com

"Poetry may make us from time to time a little more aware of the deeper, unnamed feelings which form the substratum of our being, to which we rarely penetrate; for our lives are mostly a constant evasion of ourselves."
—T.S. Eliot

"Poetry is what happens when nothing else can."
—Charles Bukowski

Contents

Introduction

The influential French poet Rimbaud used what he called a *rational disorder of the senses* in order to compose his poetry, widely regarded as works of genius. He claimed writing this way involved enormous suffering. This makes one wonder if those who shared their lives with him might have suffered as well.

In war, collateral damage includes both civilian casualties and the destruction of civilian infrastructure. It is defined under international law as "justified" when the direct military advantage is considered to be greater than the harm caused—which seems weighted in favor of those who hold power.

In relationships, collateral damage means a kind of death of the hoped-for future for those who become the debris left behind. Again, there's an inherent power imbalance.

The poems in this collection focus on some well-known poets who caused suffering and suffered themselves. Each poem is narrated by either the poet or a lover, spouse, muse, or other intimate. The biographical content is factual, based on information provided in biographies and autobiographies.

The narrators for all of these poems were real people. But their voices here are speculative, that is, imagined, invented, and therefore fictional, created in order to provide insight into the lives and works of some of our most famous and troubled 20th century poets.

T.S. Eliot
(1888-1965)

The Poet's First Wife
(Vivienne Haigh-Wood Eliot)

And when living is done
he told me one fiery night
he would like his bones
flung into my grave.

Happiness is not for me
married to a genius
happiness is for women
without a man
with a destiny.

His thick man's hands
around the lumpen knot
in my slivered throat.

He did not live with me
in this world
in our cold flat
in his mind always
the long view
at the bank
where he worked
at the pub
where he hid
searching for words
to drive his engine
into the future
with a throttle
to the core of it
all the twisted parts
buried in his past.

I withered like a grape
sucked to a raisin
sun plucked, dried out
and barren, barren.

He said he still wanted
my needles and thrusts
the pain that kept him
from a mediocre life
that kept him

brutally alive.

He was mine, he was
me and I saw me
when I met my own eyes
in his disapproving face.

He rose from our mattress
white fingers like ice
his need for renewal
like a tremble pulse
that shakes the heart
while I kept a nest
of buzzing hornets
under our empty bed
and was sane
to the point of insanity.

I was like a bag of ferrets
around my lovers' necks
Virginia Woolf said
I should let go
let Tom sing hymns
write doggerel
while I bathed my heart
in a cool, cool stream.

She took the stones
to the bottom muck
while I got manhandled
by the masters of lunacy
alone in a cage
of self-immolation.

This is *my* lament
for a fallen world:
I waited for him
at the still point
of his sad, sad heart.

The Poet's Muse
(Emily Hale)

More than a thousand
secret letters of love
my flesh still intact
his genius still abroad
intimate only
with his posterity
the artist needing solitude
in order to soar
above his muse
(me, he claimed
his *hyacinth girl*)
my wings clipped, legs
he told me once
like stuffed telephone poles.

He locked me in
his prison of devotion
his kind of faith
issued from bleakness
from invisible despair.

Despite his ejaculations
moments of deep fusion
his was a dry brain
a seasonless man, unable
to bear much reality
like unclean yellow feet
soiled hands, the stench
of a life together.

He locked himself
in a glazed mirror
a man meeting himself
masked face to face.

After I surrendered
to his reverent avoidance
he withdrew his offers
my life a sinkhole
he stepped past, blind
to my destitution
converted in his lyrics

about useful moments—
moonlight on the yew tree
the frightening beauty
cast by my memory,
and me
buried underneath
the tree of graveyards.

He locked himself in
his own oral history
wings of the future
darkened by the past
my life a touchstone
a large flat rock
he rested upon
for two decades

all alone.

The Poet's Friend
(Mary Trevelyan)

To fare forward
I told him many times
in my place beside him
Virginia Woolf dead
his wife in an asylum
his huge hands folded
in prayer beside me.

Oh la!

Nights drinking sherry
by the fire in my hearth
listening to Beethoven
cooking simple meals
he took out the rubbish
and I loved him so.

Well, well!

To my first declaration
he claimed he was recovering
from life with Vivienne.
My second love letter
he ripped, stripped, burnt
all his sadness, guilt.

Strike me pink!

It is hard for a man
to be a classic
in his own lifetime.

He bought me a car
to drive him around
to church, doctors
the pub in Paddington
The Waste Land
on our minds.

Oh la!

It is hard for a man

with a hacking cough
stooped and bent
lungs, racing heart
old before his time.

He put me in charge
of his funeral, the music
gravestone, his near end
in my capable hands.
Why should we both be lonely?

Well, well.

I thought I knew how
to handle genius
the selfishness that serves it
after fifteen years together
I thought I knew how
to love the man

'til his letter arrived:
faring forward finally
he'd eloped
with his young secretary.

Strike me pink!

The Poet's Lover
(Valerie Fletcher Eliot)

A reed with the reeds of the river
was how he would be waiting
for me, he promised
once he was dead
we had only eight
years of marriage, too short
I'd fallen in love at 14
with his poems, his voice
the voice of a god I made
my way to his side, to his desk
as his secretary I served him
faithfully, fully
I lived to tend his shrine.

A tall fleshy girl he loved
my long white limbs, naked
in high heels, I brought out
the man in the monk hidden
from those other women
I was spared, spared for him
during the war a sniper fired
on my red school cloak
a miracle I escaped, lived
to worship at his altar.

After he died I kept his things
in place: papers, ashtrays full
oxygen tanks in their spaces
love notes on a Scrabble board
romantic, erotic, stuck
prisoner of his greatness
I rescued him—and myself
he called me *a peach of a girl*
creamy, sweet, nourishing.

He erased his past for me
but I reached out to them
inviting the other women
in the long afterlife I spent
guarding his reputation
his posthumous existence

'til the moment I joined him
in the tall damp grasses
of that distant land.

Ted Hughes
(1930-1998)

The Poet's First Wife
(Sylvia Plath)

He entered my life like a continent
he wanted to inhabit, master
his way, live in his own way
London *a drab stodgy filth*
exhausted faces, exhausted streets
America *sterilized under cellophane*
—in such lyrics he talked, outlining
his plan to raise minks, run off
to Australia, taste his own roots
in the windswept land
a wilderness of a man
unlike any other he wanted
to defy the stars.

I lived within my own myth
tracking him down like prey
after reading his Grimm work
at a debauched launch
of a literary journal, jazz
dance and turtleneck sweaters
I flashed my American beach smile
drew blood when we kissed
he ripped off my red hairband
told me the memory of me
went through him like brandy
smooth, he was so smooth
told me I was first-rate
a poetess, a poet
not soft like other women
better than many good men—
defy the stars!

In touch with the primeval
a brute vitality, mystery man
of hulking bulk, earthy voice
invoking the ancient power
of dreams, night, fright, lust
I gave myself crashing, thrashing
to him, to the violent intensity
banging, blasting, ferocious love
basking in the sun of his ruthless

force he lived outside
rules, strictures, life
untamed showing me how
to write true, true
to my inner demons, weirdness
what he called beautiful, beautiful
America and he said my face
was like the wild sea, a stage
for all weathers and tidal
pulls of the moon, stars.

I taught him discipline, submitted
his work, indulging him—
six eggs whipped in hot milk
Ouija board, astrology charts
the fixed stars he believed in
consulting the tarot I found
gloomy, macabre, all worms
and whispering bones.

A primitive human animal
black panther, big man-cat
my shadow love, my equal
our life a double exposure
he called me *ponk, kish puss*
darling darling darling he said
he could crush me into his pores
he would pour into me
and fill himself with me and
kill himself on me, deep in
our kingdom of bright particles.

The Poet's Poet Wife
(Sylvia Plath)

He thought marriage a nest
of scorpions, the bloody monster
that ate up many little snakes
but I was his luck, he said
our marriage his spiritual medium
from which richness spilled forth
in bed or out we struck sparks
in our lyrical *folie à deux*.

We left urban crush and chaos
for the countryside of his youth
among creatures of wilderness
lush heather, still ponds
water-voles, a tawny owl that lit
upon his dark head
but my new position
as university teacher led to his
and we entered the rat race
in America, the beer he said
unspeakable, unspewable
like sucking old pennies
jobs that *petrified his glands*
crippling him with emotional dryness
in the buffed and glazed unnatural world
of Cadillacs, fake smiles, brash opulence
bright plastic, plastic everywhere.

Across the open sea again
to the constant cold rumble
the huge forge of London
pounding us down, down
my husband a public figure
in a windowless cell of fame
we struggled in self-anesthesia
the baby an exhaustive delight.

Our poetry followed close
on blood-sticky feet
trapped tight together
needing space to write
apart
we escaped to the moorland

14

by the river he dreamed of
a rural country home
a small hut where he could work
a greenhouse, orchard, garden
full of pheasants stalking
in bright plumes, kingfishers
thrushes, redwings, swifts
flocking on our squishy fruit
our abundance blessed again
a second child, a son.

Elemental, part of the landscape
he grew broody, slinking off
to the River Taw to fish
his new good luck charm
—not me, not anymore
I was the dead end
with my duties, distractions
babies, nappies, every meal
a gourmet production while
I withered in comparison
to the bohemian free life
with her, his archetypal witch.

What happens in the heart
simply happens, he said.

Mine fractured into shards.

My poetry carried me forth
on a bareback ride of eloquent rage
to the city, to Yeats' old home
where I wrote in a red fury
the best poems of my life
snowed in with two babies
knocked on tranquilizers
flu and frozen pipes.

He drove through a blizzard
to bring me cold potatoes
from our country garden
I knew he still cared
I was the hedgehog he loved
prickles that kept him attached.

Snowdrifts up to the windows
and me in my thin nightgown
kneeling before the oven door
deep in domestic depression
drugged on doctor's orders
taking the gas ride out.

But after the funeral
he took all the credit, pity
a mad wife, mad life
no doubt where the blame lies
the only one who could help me
transformed me into the mat
he wiped his black boots on
on his way out the door
on his way, his own way
to defy the stars.

The Poet's Lover
(Assia Wevill)

At night he hears the wolves
howling in the grass green park
her grave an ugly mouth
he falls in over and over.

He wanted to simplify
his life and write, write
but couldn't resist
the rosy lure, the golden allure
young limbs on still blue days
daffodils in bloom, the moor
rich in funk, fertile smells.

In bed we ripped flesh, slept hard
her head lodged between us
her razor blade energy slicing in
between us she became legend
while I shrunk down, toad size
an ad writer, hopping
from husband to husband
to hers and away again.

I heard the chilling howls
and the black Hanged Man
shook me to the bone.

A man sits in the desert
holding a gun with one bullet
a black bird sits in the tree—
should he shoot it
or himself?

I met him at their apartment
I sublet with my husband
a poet too, met him again
in their big thatched house
and our eyes seared hearts
and his wife knew
and his wife went mad
and she left him
and I left mine

and I raised his children
in his dead wife's home
her ice cold mausoleum.

The plum tree ripe with fruit
the first time ever he said
when I bore his child
my sweet pink girl.

He dreamed his dead wife
coming back to him
in bright reds, slashing
with her murderous art
on the moor's edge
her garden a cemetery.

But he did love me
until he didn't
I wasn't her and
all the other women
circled in for the kill.

One death infects another
and wolves howl in concert
in harmony and for pleasure
fruit ripens 'til it rots
the truth kills everybody
and I died the same way
prostrate before the gas oven
cold poison reduced to ash
our daughter's still blue arms
a garland around my neck.

The Poet's Second Wife
(Carol Orchard Hughes)

Crow threw a long black wing
over his head, he said.

First his mother passed
then his lover, child
gassed and the shadow spread.
Every man must skin his own
skunk was how he saw it.

He had to function
in the broken down factory
of domestic machinery
not writing just feeling
empty, in a stricken daze
like a fish in cold air
haunted by ghosts
of women past.

Even the pike couldn't save him
a trip to the old fishing hole
an oily dried-up puddle
yet he made a token cast
and caught the biggest perch
a metaphor he said
an ironic sign:
the old life held all rewards.

Only 17 then, up the road
I was the farmer's daughter
part Welsh, part gypsy
he saw in me a path ahead
felt his bones open again.

I babysat, nursed, mending
the wounds of his children
I could see what he needed:
help skinning his skunk
in privacy and solitude
the shadow of the Crow's wing
slowly gently lifting, lifting.

19

The Poet's Widow
(Carol Orchard Hughes)

At home on the moorland
under well-meaning clouds
breeding beef cows, fluffy sheep
beautiful beasts with my dad
the archive of farm knowhow
and he was content.

But after Dad passed we moved
back to their thatched house
Sylvia's ghost in every corner
in oaks and ash and apple trees
the wood pigeons in loud flocks
breathing in the womb of time.

I was no poet but
I was full-hearted
I loved our life
the wild peacocks and our bull
followed me across fields
he called me a wonder, light
after giant steel doors shut down
over parts of him still he was
Her Husband
trapped in their blood-jet past.

Her fame spreading
her death igniting
an uprising of hatred
tax debt from her estate
earnings swamping us
and he felt persecuted
treading a minefield
publicity like sticking electrodes
in his children's heads he said
the poison was still poison
for being fact.

He said we all own the rights
to the facts of our life
and I helped him
write, write
in privacy and solitude—

the years as Poet Laureate
decades as the people's poet
deerstalking with Prince Charles
fishing with the Queen
world travels, readings, fans
my blind eye to his follies
mistresses, sub-mistresses
while I gardened, cooked, hosted
stability
so he could give voice
to pain, reconciling it
with the rest of the civilized world.

After he died a lion
ran loose in the moors
leaving a large paw print
near the river bed.

I encouraged my husband
to put himself first, poetry
above all else including me
and he did love me
not most, but longest
lady, he said
are you satisfied
—and I was.

Edna St. Vincent Millay
(1892-1950)

The Poet's Mother
(Cora Millay)

I shed their father
like skin off a chicken
moved my three girls
relative to relative
the grace of Maine
took pity on us
with a rustic cabin
overlooking the river
in small-town Camden.

Dirt poor and skilled
nursing took me away
for weeks at a time
to care for the sick
my eldest girl
responsible, reliable
Edna in charge.

She preferred Vincent
my pretty little elf
her autumn glory hair
cascading to her feet
mellow voice, rich language
scooped from my big trunk
of classic books—Shakespeare,
Milton, Keats, plays and recitals
I missed so much
she missed me so.

At home I wove hair
for women's wigs
stitching all night long
in the one heated room
Vincent often bedridden
I healed her myself
with fresh sea water
baths, broths, massage.

I taught all my girls
the strong woman's truth:
no need for a man
when you're loved at home.

The Poet's Suitors
(Camden High boys)

If this be love
I've had enough of it
the kind of thing she said
after you brought her to paradise
showed her a good time
recited classic poetry
leaned in for a kiss.

Respect thyself, be worthy
of thine own respect
her made-up commandments
she didn't respect us
none of us top boys
could get anywhere with her
or best her in class
or win prizes at school.

For one thing is certain,
I can't stand this long
no wonder we turned
ganged up on her
made her suffer, lose
the Class Poet award.

Humiliated and enraged
she dropped out of school
mocked and scorned
oh how we laughed!

But she laughed last
the first woman to win
the Pulitzer Prize
for Poetry.

The Poet's Female Lovers
(Vassar girls)

She dreamed of a house
white with green trim
a man to rescue her
from duty, drudgery
hands red and swollen
washing, scrubbing, cooking
while beauty meant more
than anything else
but she had no time
to be a pretty girl

in her backwoods town
a rich patron
spotted her genius
and away Vincent flew
to a new nest of women
in the dorm, her classes
we all adored her
slept cuddled, exploring
her bold softness
fighting over her

our rising star
role model of rebellion
smoking in cemeteries
cutting class, chapel
playing
by her own rules
she had the power
to make everyone fall
in love with her.

The Poet's Male Lovers
(Arthur Hooley, Salomón de la Selve, Edmund Wilson)

If sex were a poison
she would *sip it*
drop by drop she said
until she could *enjoy it more*
than anyone alive and me
I taught her how
to get in
and get out
fast, heart intact.

I was a mystery
she wanted to solve
a gloomy distant moon
I called her *child*
her androgyny appealed
I held her, held her
at bay.

Still, she pined for me
and I inspired her
to be the jaded romantic
the relatable ironic poet
she became famous for
celebrity, wisdom, sex
after me she was always
the one in control.

*

Spanish and hot-blooded
passion overwhelming
I wooed her, full of her
everywhere I went
she was inside me
a precious wine
dizzying, her spell.

I came to New York City
escorted her everywhere
the opera, galas, soirées
introduced her to patrons

editors who bedded her
but only I knew her
heart pregnant with sadness
a deep dark loneliness
no man could erase.

*

We met at a party
after I'd praised her
fine work in print
I knew she burned
the candle at both ends
a bohemian life
shimmering in batik
my first lover, love
of my life
never mine.

I made the mistake
of sharing her
with a friend
in bed my heart
flayed, shredded.

All that adoration
made her appear
both human and divine
her supernatural beauty
in a long gauzy dress
flowing princess train
floating there
above her little gold slippers
an angel sent down
from the heavens above
for us to love

but only from afar.

The Poet's Husband
(Eugen Boissevain)

We lived for each other
for the glory of art
vowing forever love
free and unpossessive
life with a renowned poet
of the erotic impulse
voice of the erotic condition
I came after cocktail party fame.

I came after all the lovers
actresses, writers, bisexual
gay and straight, everyone
mesmerized by her beauty
enthralled by her verse.

I came after the abortion
her mother gave her
that herbal concoction
made her so ill
for four years
I tended her like a wife.

I came after Paris
and all the sex
and all the parties
and the exhaustion
the depression that broke her
fragile bird, wingless
and my analyst Jung
showed me how to help.

I came to her bedside
fed her, read to her
wrote her correspondence
bought her clothes, cars
a giant emerald ring—
nothing too good for her
and our marriage
and our sanctuary
an old blueberry farm

we called Steepletop
seven hundred wooded acres
I turned into a farm, a garden
jasmine, daisies, columbine
red roses and pennyroyal
for my beautiful wife.

The Poet's Last Lover
(George Dillon)

She penned the poetry
of savage desire and I
fellow Pulitzer poet
but younger, so green
she couldn't turn her back on
the most beautiful thing:
her passion aflame.

We ran off in Paris
left her poor husband
her last season of love
inspiring her to write
the pain and beauty
ripping at her throat
more violently
than death.

After her mother died
she courted oblivion:
alcohol, pills, and sex
with me while her husband
jumped into the Seine
to rescue some girl.

A hero like that
and she let him sail
back to New York
alone.

The Poet's Last Love
(Morpheus)

Eugen would do anything
to keep her he purchased
their very own island
off the Maine coast
to spend naked days
in the frothy seafoam chill
catching lobster, cooking chowder
warming on sun-baked rocks
her beauty fading with age
alcohol and Seconal, cocaine
hash, and me:
Morpheus, she said
she loved me
she had no shame
she loved badly
she could no longer write.

After years in a rocker
in a rumpled housedress
shooting me every hour
she got treatment
she dumped me
like all her lovers
cleaned up on the island
devoted to her devoted
husband they spent days
reading as ocean waves
lapped their loose flesh.

He died so fast
she fell in
the soft haze of forgetting
she fell down
the stairs at Steepletop
their ashes side-by-side
under pines and hemlock
two candles burning
in forever love.

Dylan Thomas
(1914-1953)

The Poet's Wife
(Caitlin Macnamara Thomas)

He blew the bones
out of the hills, the sky
brightened for everyone
while I stood by, waiting
the lonely leftover wife
of a famous artist, yes
I had to have him
his heart of a werewolf
full of worms, needles, thorns
until he died young
from drink.

He wrapped the tame
in the wild convolutions
of his eccentric mind
a complicated way
of communicating
filtered through Welsh
country life, humor
with a special injection
of Celtic energy
he made the biggest lies
sound true
only after drinking
all day all night
did the devil's truth
come out.

A public barbarian
in private sensitive
his writing he said
reconciled the conflict
(*a beast, an angel, and a madman in me*)
and his forever themes
birth, death, decay
the rot in life
he said he struggled
through his writings
from darkness
to some measure
of light.

He was weak, decadent
I was drunk, hostile
we had no money
dressed in rags
I made him shirts
cut from curtains
we stole
from our friend's homes
their money, good wine
I cooked his mother's food:
faggots and peas
tripe and leeks
laver bread
(the bread of the sea)
spread with cockles
and salted butter.

He read for the BBC, wrote
scripts, radio plays, illustrated
little maps of the islands
on his *two-tongued sea*
his intellectual gifts
hidden at the pub
a man of the people
secret life in a shack
where he sat, smoking
writing down to death.

I wanted to write too
of the ice-cream hills
the crackling black sea
the nutcracker bar hounds
with their taproom noses
but when I asked how
he said
you either feel it
or you can't
and I couldn't
I was always drunk
pregnant, on edge
sweet as a razor, he said
a *needling stalactite hag*.

While I washed the dishes
or cleaned up his messes
he'd recite his long poems—
the *seasaw sea, sloeback*
crowblack fishingboatbobbing sea—
I couldn't even listen,
made no sense to me
I was afraid
I would drown
in his ocean
of words.

Drink was his temporary escape
from the slavery of his calling
there was no escape
for me
from Dylan
his werewolf heart
full of black blood
until he died
from drink.

The Poet's Drinking Partner
(Caitlin Macnamara Thomas)

Our story is a love story
a love of drink story.

We were always in pubs
too young I fell for him
at the local bar
our natural habitat
he talked nonstop
drank nonstop, fifteen
twenty pints a day
black and tans
bitter and milds
his appetite for Guinness
mine for Scotch and ginger
whiskey, more and more

we were the same
sops, lazy, bohemian
sloppy and poor
The Two Terrible Children
they called us until
we had three of our own
moved to South Wales
the sea-end of town
the long tan miles
of mud and sand
wave-carved rocks
lowering skies

we settled in
the Boat House
four levels of rustic
rope-railings, widow's walks
the crawl of wild roses
the tide roaring in
sweeping children out
while we were off
drinking
at Brown's Hotel
and pub.

I was always in pubs
grew up in an inn
my father a blarney-man, poet
of inferior talent my mother
French, classy, neglectful
I discovered drink, ran off
with my father's friend
a famous painter I modeled
for the old man always
looking for him
in all the men I met

Dylan had that same charm
and immense talent, a way
with people, people everywhere
loved him, not me
this truth
magnified by
his growing importance
my growing unimportance
our shared Irish sickness.

We were always wasted
the sun bulldozing
our booze-bleary eyes
we were always broke
money down the drain
of drink, his patrons'
money down the hatch
my big, fat, cunning slice
of Welsh storytelling
could wheedle and woo
the free drinks until
we went to bed drunk
passed out, got up
hung over
to do it all over
with renewed vigor.

Our love story
a love of drink story
the pub our altar
we worshipped daily
two lovers
of the drink.

The Poet's Widow
(Caitlin Macnamara Thomas)

I lived in the shadow
of his throbbing
cavernous voice, his rib
rumbling penetrating
the heart
of Liberty Land
of '50s America
I couldn't wait
to leave that bloody country
never to return, he went
back three times—
the last time
fatal.

His literary reputation
not his pudgy troll looks
brought opportunities
glamorous famous
celebrities, parties, women
so to save face
I went out on my own
my *hotwaterbottle body*
snapped up by locals
my rustic conquests
could not stand up
to his worldly affairs
I felt reduced
to a minor role
I was not destined
to play.

Happy at home
in his writing shed
his hideaway hut
dusty green walls
empty beer bottles
tall piles of ash
two big windows
overlooking the rush
of water to the Irish Sea
overlooking the estuary
the cormorants drying wings

lithe herons stabbing fish
curlews and hawks circling
birds the color of red flannel.

Living out the poet legend
he expected to be poor
he expected to die young
he expected me to swallow
in silence
the raw red bleeding meat
of our marriage
our fights legendary:
we wrestled on floors
he threw a book at me
he threw a knife at me
I attacked, he defended
I hit him with a torch
knocked him out
burnt one woman
with my cigarette
knocked another one
broke her skinny arm.

On that final trip
to New York success
had him by the throat
his schedule grueling
his body weakened
a doctor gave him
drugs, injections
Benzedrine, morphine
until he collapsed

on a hospital bed slowly
fading away, approaching
his own good night

when I arrived drunk
to the deathly silence
his thrilling voice still
of course I freaked
fell upon his limp body
banged my head on glass
tore down a crucifix

got shipped to Bellevue
while he went out
with a whimper.

On the ship home
I drank five doubles
trashed the bar until
the captain tossed me
into the hold
with the body
with my husband
finally alone
together
where we belonged.

The Poet's American Lovers
(too many to name)

We wanted him because he was Dylan
a cute and cuddly animal
intimate and impossible
stimulating and explosive
a pacifist who brawled in bars
a moral man who ditched his bills
borrowed and never paid back.

We wanted him because he was famous
sincere but tactless, no humility
no discretion he would jump in
a soft bread-pudding bed
with any one of us, all of us
waiting at the Chelsea Hotel
hanging at the White Horse Tavern
we worshipped him
loved, lost, hated him.

We loved him because he was a poet
uninhibited and theatrical
purveyor of rural romanticism
conveyor of a waterfall of words
that touched the subconscious
that bridged the dreary gap
between war-weary modernism
and glittering multicolor pop
between art and performance art
academic literature and a verse
that spoke to the rest of us.

We wanted to drown ourselves
in his ocean
of words.

We loved him because he was sick
with all of our griefs in his arms
seedy with bottomless drink
swimming toward darkness
he warned us all
death before forty—
and he was right
about dying young.

Robert Lowell
(1917-1977)

The Poet's First Love
(Anne Dick)

It was the happiest year
of my life I told my analyst
Bobby was my cousin's friend
brooding, brilliant, six years
younger, my way out
of a debutante world
of showing a face not mine
in those days until Bobby
made me feel loved.

I drove us around town
he had to think, compose
poems I thought bad
wretched little things
he brought so much life
to my parents' dinner table
my staid home near his
Brahmin Boston's
uptight Beacon Hill
the rain-wet cobblestones
beneath expensive boots
of blue blood bores
we rebelled against
their old-fashioned mores
and lack of morality.

Bobby always told me
I looked like Bette Davis
the big eyes, round
face, pretty enough
I think
he loved me, promised
to drop out of Harvard
and elope to Europe
until his mother threatened
to take his funds away
shared his letters
with a corrupt psychiatrist
who did her bidding
who committed my Bobby
to an insane asylum.

He had cat eyes yellow-
green, high cheekbones
his muscular body
perfectly sculpted, tall
model handsome, smart
but quite lost
in the world of reality
his lovable helplessness
made women want
to nurture and heal
and he left behind
a smoking trail
of women like me
our lives changed
impassioned, inspired but
we were all damaged, hurt
we all wanted him still.

Bobby transferred colleges
escaped his mother's clutches
sent me a dear John letter
ruined my life and
I kept the ruin going
married a teenager, drank
cycled through hospitals
and hung myself
with theater curtain ropes
in a dramatic final act.

It was the happiest year
of my life.

The Poet's First Wife
(Jean Stafford)

He learned to be a brute
at boarding school
the big boys beat
the small boys while
the old men watched
fondly, he said
from the wings.

He learned in school
he was bigger, stronger
his own raw power
fist fighting his friends
menacing his enemies
impressing his teachers
with the exotic language
of an emotional wildman.

Spending time in the South
he learned how to speak
how to smooth a drawl
in his Boston accent
how to ease into a story
like there's a peach
in your mouth.

Eventually he also learned
to be less burly and surly
to be fun, witty, unaffected
take a bath, trim his hair
to use the poet's charisma
to charm all kinds
of women like me.

He learned from poets,
writers his role models
of the male prerogative:
move from wife to wife
and maintain a string
of desperate mistresses
in emotional distress—
which he did with me
repeatedly.

And repeatedly
I took him back
I thought I could
fix him, fix me, stop
drinking, stay sane
I was always afraid
of what he would do
hands around my throat
driving drunk smashing up
my face, a punch there
rebroke my poor nose
he said I breathed too much!

My murderer-poet.

Eventually he left me
our wooded Maine home
I wanted to die, die
in the mental hospital
reading his poems
about me
so cruel, hateful.

A bestselling author
proud of my success
I'd lost my way
with him and
he'd learned too well
how to ruin everything
for a woman
like me.

The Poet's Second Wife
(Elizabeth Hardwick)

Honey, it's just too
boring but guess what
I was the stable platform
he rested upon
in between the chaos
of two unstable wives
multiple breakdowns
countless affairs and fights
jail time and mental hospitals.

I had the right grit
Kentucky born, raised
in a pack of wild kids
in small town America
I had drive, ambition
success as a writer
I fell for him
like all the others
he fell for me
in a manic love state.

I was often frightened
for my safety, the safety
of our young daughter
he said he felt flayed
tortured by disruptive patterns
of mental excess and exuberance
followed by guilt, shame, exhaustion
in five countries at fifteen hospitals,
clinics, drugs, electroshock, analysis
nothing
worked he was
who he was.

I believed in him
and guess what
he kept coming back
he said he was frightened
he was always afraid
he'd be permanently insane
honey, it's just too
sad.

The Poet's Collaborating Muse
(Elizabeth Hardwick)

Why not say what happened:
he used my letters, my words
to prop up his masterpiece
in which I was abused
the tossed aside old wife
for one younger, prettier
much *much* wealthier

I became what I dreaded
a symbol, feminist icon
for the dumped wife
no longer his muse
cast aside after decades
as the glamorous couple
center of the literary glitterati.

He no longer lay
all day stretched out
on our tousled bed
smoking, drinking
from bottles of milk
or escaping to attend
conferences and workshops
readings and after-parties
serial affairs and adventures
while I managed our home
raised our daughter
wrote bestselling novels.

He said poems lie
he lied to me.

He brought home one
beautiful young girl
when I was fat and forty
he escorted other girls
to plays, museums, dinners
leased apartments for them
proposed marriage, gave them
rings, his death do we part
love he claimed
I crashed over his head

49

like a merciless sea.

When he left me for the heiress
I took all I could:
his annual trust fund
the apartment in New York
the house in Maine
his first edition books
his family silver.

Why not say what happened:
he believed in his words
the authenticity of his suffering
as much more valuable
than my deep anguish.

The Poet's Women Friends
(Mary McCarthy, Elizabeth Bishop)

We thought he was generous
a gentleman, genteel
welcoming us to his home
his chaotic world, his thinking
the gush of genius, a peek
inside his personal hell.

We found him helpful
to our careers, our writing
because he loved us
believed in us
introduced us
to editors, benefactors
got us readings, contracts
teaching positions, publishers
praised us publicly
loyal to the end.

We agreed he was supportive
overlooking our failings
our criticisms, jealousies, sniping
depressions and divorces
breakdowns and drinking bouts
he was understanding
he was inspirational
when he was not
too sedated
too manic
too crazed.

He was modest
about his impact
his impressive output
his tumultuous narrative
his homes, lovers, wives
shuffling family
sacrificing sanity
to create, his life
a razor's edge
an autobiography
of a hallucination.

The Poet's Third Wife
(Lady Caroline Blackwood)

My mind's not right
he said many times
mad, bad, and dangerous
to know, that was Robert
I felt that way too
painfully shy, often silent
for hours, days I needed
drink to set my tongue
rattling and seething
pen to paper, writing
as my ancestors had:
in the veins of the Irish
blood tingles like champagne.

My mother's Guinness genes
ancestral brewers, bankers
poets, playwrights, politicians
movers and shakers, eccentrics
drunks she inherited wit
wore plastic platform shoes
with live goldfish in the heels
while us kids ran wild
over three thousand acres
fell off horses, broke bones
never set, never right
one creepy horse groomer
gave me pills, pills
I was a child riding
like a man, learning
about the power
a girl can wield.

Lady Caroline the desirable
debutante and heiress
to the Guinness estate
crumbling moldy walls
cold floors, scuttling mice
I grew up surrounded
by Victorian plunder—
a blackened rhino head
a mummified Egyptian hand
cutlasses, pistols, spiked balls

a manmade lake
in the shape of a shamrock—
my father handsome, admired
Under Secretary for the Colonies,
Speaker for the Senate
of Northern Ireland
racking up gambling debt
running off to war
never to return.

My life governed
by the dark curse
of the Guinness line
I kept up a frantic pace
lovers, parties, scandals
husbands who never lasted
three children, divorced
after Robert moved in
we had a son, our kids
living in our ruins
our grand squalor
Robert's insanity
triggering my own.

I ran away, escaping
into vodka
whenever he was manic
I couldn't help
my breathless panic
suicidal thoughts
our emotions compounded
our lives heightened
yet paralyzed too
whenever he freelanced
in the kingdom of the mad.

Our minds were not right
due to aristocratic upbringings
and too much interbreeding
poor little rich twins
we'd hitched our halters
thoroughbred mental cases
riding into a dark future
together, alone.

The Poet's Widow
(Caroline Blackwood)

It's the worst, being left
not knowing
if he would return
if he'd lived
if he would've left her
again
after he left me
in rural Ireland
said he missed
our big winey dinners
in our big rotting house
while he taught at Harvard
he went back to her
in New York City
his second wife
her ability to care
when he was lost
he took a taxi
from the airport
in his arms
a painting of me
he clutched it
as if he would never
let me go.

After years of warning
he wouldn't make it
to 60 he turned 60
a fatal heart attack
in the backseat
of the yellow cab
by then he felt
fizzled, stale, small.

It's the worst to see
a man, a woman, an estate
soaked in the black suds
of disaster and sold off
to help pay off
debt, help, rooms
rented out while I wrote
of the abyss he fell in
without me.

Elizabeth Bishop
(1911-1979)

Elizabeth Bishop on Elizabeth Bishop

My life was one
of words and whiskey
deep contemplation
keen observation
of nature and people
farmers and factory workers
fishermen, fish, the Amazon
jungle, the beach
lovers, birds, moose
all around me life—
difficult, full of joy.

I was born to wealth
New England bluenose
world of privilege

until my father died
I was 8 months old
my mother unraveling
left me with her parents
in a Nova Scotia village
where I grew up happy
running around barefoot
taking the cow to pasture
past gabled wood houses
low hills, tall elms, leaning
willows and kind villagers

until my father's parents
horrified by my wildness
took me to Massachusetts
their cold city manse
and mean Uncle Jack
picked on and teased me
unhappy, unwell
asthmatic, homesick

until my grandfather sent me
to breathe the ocean air
with dear Aunt Maud
and I read read read
in my little sickbed
and I fell in love
with the Victorian poets.

Maud's husband a sadist
abused us, hit, groped
at an early age
I learned about men
who would hurt you
if you let them—
after that
I never did.

Elizabeth Bishop on Her Thirst

A baby in a crib
at my dead father's
family summer home
on the bay
at Marblehead Neck
the Great Salem Fire
bringing in boats
frightened survivors
a red sky, intense heat.

Awake, alone, afraid
all that night
I cried for my mother
thirsty and scared
but she did not come
I could see out the window
she stood in the front yard
white dress rosy from fire
billowing in the heat
serving coffee and food
thousands left homeless
one thousand dead.

Alone, awake, afraid
all night I called out
thirsty and scared
but nobody came.

I grew up without her
and went off to college
learned about drinking
numbing my feelings
for the rest of my life
I drank and I drank
it was never enough
still thirsty and scared.

The Poet's College "Friend"
(Louise Crane)

We met at Vassar where
I struggled, she excelled
I dropped out, she won honors
and we stayed in touch
in New York City
traveling around Europe
deep-sea fishing in Florida
where one time she caught
a 65-pound amberjack.

She'd had this boyfriend
on crutches from polio
a Harvard business grad
fell for her, invited her
for romantic island trysts
on Nantucket, Cuttyhunk
pinned her, begged her
to marry him
to no avail
he became suicidal
sent her a postcard:
Elizabeth, Go to hell
then killed himself
proved to her
one more tragic time
men could not
be counted on
to be safe.

I could match her
drink for drink
and care for her
when she fell ill
my widowed mother
a paper company heiress
paid for our travel
a Paris apartment
seven lovely rooms
a maid, a cook, a car
accident when I drove
our Vassar friend
a talented painter

her one arm severed
at the elbow.

Elizabeth fell in love
with the lushness of Florida
swamps, palm forests
strange beautiful birds
the island of Key West
a quiet, simple village
I bought her a house there
with a shaded front porch
banana, mango, lime trees.

I left her there
for New York, other lovers
her poetry her only
consistent lifelong love
her means of illumination
her fear of mental illness
the drive to write
poems to protect herself,
her own rational mind.

The Poet's Fling
(Marjorie Carr Stevens)

I moved to Key West
to recover my health
leaving my husband
in Boston, his idea
of open marriage
I did not want until
I met Elizabeth.

A funny girl with thick
unruly hair
short, plump, pretty
shy, elusive, fortified
on alcohol we were both
so drunk when we met
she fell off her bicycle
she took me home
to her empty white house
she moved in with me
behind the Caroline Shop
owned by Pauline Hemingway
and her gay sister.

To escape the Navy men
flocking the island
during the war
we went to Mexico
we lived in New York
then back to Key West
that beautiful paradise
paper-white in moonlight
jade pools, pearl sand
we were in love
with the easy island life

until she started
drinking whiskey
earlier and earlier
in the long hot days
she fell in love easily
fell out easily too.

The Poet's "Lota"
(Maria Carlotta de Macedo Soares)

A driven designer
from an aristocratic family
from Rio de Janeiro
when I first met Elizabeth
in New York I fell for her
but I was with my girlfriend.

Four years later Elizabeth came
to my city she fell in love
with the smell of coffee
brewing in the cafés
my rooftop apartment
above Copacabana beach
girls in bright bathing suits
handsome men walking dogs
and in the misty distance
the black granite cliffs
blooming orchids, waterfalls
in the mountains where
I was building a glass house
I called *Samambaia.*

She took two bites
of our sour cashew fruit
and got *cajun* poisoning
a violent allergic reaction
her face, hands swelled up
and I nursed her
and built her a studio
so she wouldn't leave me
and she didn't
for fifteen years.

She was a rare bird
fluttering in my hands
a Pulitzer Prize winner
and the poet laureate
living alone in D.C.
when the government purged
all homosexual employees
frightened, closeted
she drank and dried out
multiple times.

I dammed a waterfall
she swam in the pool
trekked up the hills
and worked steadily
creating from her past
exorcizing her demons

until the demons in us
destroyed what we'd built.

Lota's Friend
(Lilli Correia de Arújo)

Lota was summoned
away from their home
to live in Rio
to spearhead a massive
public works project
in Copacabana
above the sultry beach
Elizabeth cooked meals
typed Lota's paperwork
entertained and assisted
but she could not write
and she was drinking
behind Lota's back.

So Lota brought her
to my home in Ouro Pètro
a historic Portuguese town
full of baroque buildings
a quiet artists' haven
Elizabeth longed for
she could not tolerate
all the drama, fighting
with my old friend Lota
so stressed and angry
with her project delays

Elizabeth finally fled
into my soothing arms.
I never told Lota.

Elizabeth met Roxanne
a young pregnant girl
married to an artist
and Lota found out
went completely mad
was institutionalized
raging and blaming
Elizabeth in New York
when Lota visited her
overmedicated, overdosed
her way to say goodbye.

The Poet's Assistant
(Roxanne Cummings)

I was called by her doctor
to help her recover
after a fall down the stairs
her world gone flat
after Lota's suicide
so I flew from Seattle
to work as her secretary.

We lived in New York
we moved out to Frisco
we moved to Brazil
and she worked steadily
thinking her feelings
she called writing poems
while I mined the rocks
hammering them apart
for diamonds and gold

my mind breaking down
old story of my life
I had to be hospitalized
I had to be sent home
another mental case
leaving Elizabeth
swamped again
by the black waves
of regret and shame

all alone she was
sinking, sinking
in the solo swirl
of poetry and alcohol
her twin compulsions
her organizing principles
more powerful for her
than love.

The Poet's Young "Friend"
(Alice Methfessel)

When her best buddy
the poet Robert Lowell
left Boston for England
Elizabeth taught his classes
the first woman teacher
of advanced writing
in Harvard history.

She lived in Cambridge
in the visiting scholar suite
in the student dormitory
where I was the secretary
sensible, practical, not neurotic
but just 26
to her 59
I fell for her anyway
her hoarse smoker's voice
with that upper crust
New England accent
her soft manner, bright
eyes, mind, humor
we had so much to say
and we bridged
our generation gap
with care.

She felt at home here
where she was born
where her family built
the Boston Public Library
the Museum of Fine Arts
in my cheerful studio
I kept her happy, writing
she said having me
in her life
was like being
in a plane
when it rises
above heavy clouds
into sunny skies.

She bought a harbor condo
with exposed brick walls
on the remodeled wharf
a view across the bay
a walk to the North End
on cobblestone streets
Italian bakeries, fish markets
fresh olive oil, red wine
but she was living on
diet drinks, cigarettes
coffee and Nembutal
and too much whiskey.

The futility of the pattern
her broken promises
to drink less
made me leave her
for a man
I planned to marry
but didn't
because I loved her.

We sat out on her balcony
above the dark winter water
sparkling blue in spring
white sailboats in summer
pumpkin-orange sunsets
in the chill fall air
I found her on the floor
not from drink
not this time
no longer thirsty
no longer scared.

LeRoi Jones
(1934-2014)

The Poet's First Wife
(Hettie Cohen Jones)

I was married to an anti-Semite
even though I was Jewish
I was married to a man
who said white women
should get raped
by black men
who were owed
by the white man
by the unjust system
steel balloons he said
tied to their mouths.

I was married to a poet
who changed his name
his philosophies, alignments
from jokester to intellectual
to anti-academic to activist
to black nationalist
to Muslim to Marxist
to full-blown conspiracy theorist
strumming his head
for a living
he said.

When I met him he was funny
a bohemian liberal hedonist
apolitical lover boy
dabbler in drugs, drinker
out-all-night type guy
until he changed
to a different man.

Suddenly I was married
to a black supremacist
angry, full of hatred
advising black men
to aid in the destruction
of white America, all
those who make money
from war, fear, and lies
who want the world
like it is, not
as it should be.

I could see his point
until it turned on me
my life raw at the edges
my anger on a tight rope
binding me down
for too many years.

I was tied up with a writer
who wanted his poems to kill
his plays to cause uproar
his essays to incite
he chipped, shot up
gave me his hepatitis
gave me his work
as his secretary
as the mother of his children
homemaker for his friends
I fed poverty salads
made spaghetti for a hundred.

Labeled a hypocrite
talking black
marrying white
cheating white
a brown baby
with a white mistress
hating me
while accusing me
of Jewish self-hatred
climbing the success ladder
while calling out
what he sought:
the great
white
American dream.

I finally left the man
who asked me
how he could be
married to the enemy
and who deserted me
our two little girls
refusing to admit
poverty wasn't black
poverty looked like me.

The Poet's Ex
(Hettie Cohen Jones)

We bonded at work
on a music magazine
this jazzy wiry dude
kind, good-humored, fun
he liked to laugh
vault fire hydrants
parking meters
laugh the loudest
in the theaters we liked
plays, playing, poetry
poets so we founded
an underground press
publishing the Beats
Ginsberg wore our couch
on his head like a hat
Kerouac our shy friend
Frank O'Hara, the painters
all drinking at our place
exploring abstract worlds.

A mixed race romance
in the '50s and '60s
despised, dangerous
we had to be tough
his family accepted me—
smart, strong, hardworking
his parents more educated
more middle class than my own
beloved Jewish bigots
leery of the young black man
in love with their daughter.

Loving him I lost
my dad
declared me dead
I lost
my way
the girl with ambition
became the woman behind
the man with ambition
I sat smiling, quiet

a shadow of myself
wanting to know how
to make myself happen
I had just begun
to make myself up.

After we split up
I gave myself voice
a desk, a space
a pen replaced him
and I wrote
children's books
editing, anthologizing
watching my ex
try on different hats
changing his face
beaten, bloodied
sometimes behind bars.

He was not in my life
never spoke to me again
but he wrote about me
how *significant* it was
that the white woman had not
produced a boy child, only girls
a man always in the news
feared, hated, loved
he opened the doors
to theatre, arts, publishing
and the Black Arts Movement
he helped establish
has never stopped.

The Poet's Second Wife
(Sylvia Robinson)

I grew up in Newark
with my grandparents
blues musicians, activists
taught me to think
speak out, be present
to sing and dance
a community organizer
all my life.

As a young woman
I had a part in a play
written by LeRoi Jones
I knew what I was doing
when I slept with the man
living with a pregnant girl
who took sick and died.

When I met him he was LeRoi
formerly Everett Leroy Jones
then Leroy Jones
then LeRoi Jones
'til he joined the Karenga
cult of African liberation
Sunni Muslims from LA
changed our names:
mine to Amina
(*faithful* in Swahili)
his to Amiri Baraka
(*blessed prince*).

He'd grown up in Newark
in a mixed neighborhood
bussed to high school
surrounded by white kids
isolated, invisible, glass
between them and he tried
to see through the wall
of his separation from girls
learned how to lust
after the abstract white life.

He rented a big house
made the first floor a theater
and launched a newspaper
in the heart of Newark
he evolved, vocal leader
of the city's black majority
and founded Spirit House
artists' residence, meeting place
the Spirit House kids
running through alleys
looking for racists to beat.

I was not a convert
but wore the dress of Islam
in which all women were
submissive, feminine, fertile—
the things LeRoi espoused!

We fought, I pressed him
to drop out of the university
of false blackness
I pushed him on
women's right to speak
he continued to rabble-rouse
to oppress the oppressed
his vitriol unacceptable
to me, to many women
and to the powers that be.

In my mind he was still
a middle class bohemian
the black boy wanting
what white America had.

The Poet's Widow
(Amina Baraka)

Amiri never understood
me, he never knew
what it was like
for working class America.

He was petty bourgeoisie
middle-class easy street
thought he was poor
with his house key
'round his neck
but he grew up comfy
played sports, trumpet
hip clothes bebopper
never part of the ugly
American ghetto.

By the time he turned 40
he was rejected, hopeless
he couldn't get published
with his loud calls
for black artists
to aid in the destruction
of (racist) America.

He'd wasted *my* life
dominating and silencing
while he tried to destroy
what he called evil:
the Fascist Bureau of Intimidation
the Crazed Imperialist Assassins
the church of specific reality
but he didn't call himself out
for cheating on me
for putting politics first
for neglecting his children
dismissing, exposing them
to harassment, terror.

No, he blew us up
over and over, yeah:
Amiri Baraka the man
who blew up America.

Anne Sexton
(1928-1974)

The Poet's Poet Friend
(Maxine Kumin)

Neighbors in the 1950s
housewives, mothers
with young children
in a Boston suburb
we didn't want to chitchat
we didn't want to gossip
we wanted to be poets
write great books
kindred spirits
ambitious women
at odds with the times.

By 1961 we were "equivalents"
in the Premier Cru, first group
of special female fellows
at the Institute for Independent Study
at Radcliffe College
an experimental program
paying a nice stipend
for two dozen women
scholars, writers, artists
to achieve something new:
to balance the tension
between art and life
between career and family
women on the cusp
of full liberation.

For two years we each
had an office to escape
husbands, housework, kids
for the perfumed rabbit warren
in an old yellow house
in lively Harvard Square
in an era of change
for women restricted, repressed
our creativity in chains
our minds dulled
by routine, boredom, cocktail hours.

When we first met
Anne was jittery, loose
fresh off a suicide attempt
new at writing poetry
entering my quiet life
like a tornado
shaking it up—
and it needed shaking:
I was writing ditties
shucking oysters, sucking gin
she gave me wildness
pulling me out
of my hard hermit shell.

Anne carried herself
like an actress
tall, thin, glamorous
edgy and seductive
like a caged tiger
she said, clawing the bars
of her conventional life
she broke taboos
she reminded us all
we couldn't rely on
white picket fences
to keep nightmares out.

The Poet's Husband
(Alfred "Kayo" Muller Sexton II)

Anne was all about Anne
spoiled rich daughter
of my boss, a pushy salesman
a drinker, red-faced bully
with a wife from hell.
They loved, ruined her
I mopped up the mess.

A woman without purpose
not a good housewife
too self-involved
to mother her own children
(my mother had to step in)
avoiding us by writing
at that fancy Institute
at snooty Radcliffe
spending the stipend
on a private study, a pool
so she could sun, swim.

When her back ached
after hours spent hunched
over some poem, no dinner
waiting on the stove
when I got home
I gave a massage
I brought her an office chair
I tried to be supportive
of her dabbling, her hobby
her games with the poets
but sometimes I couldn't
and was forced to fists
to stop her madness.

Dark, sultry, lanky Anne
getting loaded at the Ritz
three or four martinis
arriving home late
reeking of booze, cheap motels
and later an abortion, unsure
the child was mine.

After she hit the big-time
with readings, books, prizes
her ego swelled up
trying to write like a man
hanging around like a hipster
in swingin' Harvard Square
getting into trouble
flitting around Europe
romancing the Italians
on a grant the poets gave her
cash, a Pulitzer too.

Anne kept running away
deserting her family
her responsibilities
as wife and mother
days in the loony bin
on the road, in other beds
on the couch with her shrink
our marital Pearl Harbor
continually blowing up
'til she quit for good.

I could have told her
warned her how running
alone, scared
she'd resort to numbing
drinking, pills, seeking
what she liked to call
the woman's way out

one autumn afternoon
she put on her mother's fur
took a tall glass of vodka
out to the garage
sat in the car
the radio on
the engine running
and running
'til it ran out of gas.

The Poet's Therapist
(Dr. Martin Orne)

Yes, I was blamed
for the controversy
over the biography
based on the audio,
more than 300 tapes
of my private therapy
over eight years' time
with Anne Sexton.

Yes, my mother was
her therapist first
at Westwood Lodge
when she ran around
on her young husband
craving hot romance
and action, action.

I was the one who
she later wrote
walked from breakfast
to madness
at *the sad hotel*
while she raged in her own
glass bowl, thrusting
for *the old butcher*
dying to die
one of my first
long-term patients
a frustrating woman
in love with death.

I was green, she was
suicidal, together
we learned to tolerate
my mistakes, her acting
impossible, pushing off
the world of reality
we agreed to record
our therapy sessions
so she could listen after
and try to remember

and try to understand
what we'd discussed.

I tried to help with
her torrid affairs
her Salem cigarettes
her extra-dry martinis
her pocketbook of pills
the actress, performer
unable to play
the good '50s housewife
I suggested she write.

And Anne lit up
like I'd given her a shot
of insulin, electrodes
in what she once called
her *black banana brain*
she sprang up, took off
went into action, action
writing her feelings
writing her poems
a passion, a talent
a genius at work.

So yes, I encouraged her
to read the best poets
attend workshops, classes
keep writing her poems
keep staying alive, I said:
You can't kill yourself,
you have something to give.

But no, I couldn't
save her once
I saw her grow old
on her bitterness
after I left Boston
the support system
that kept Anne alive
all those years
ruptured, collapsed
and yes, yes

I do blame myself.

The Poet's Last Friend
(Maxine Kumin)

I knew she would leave me
someday
but not that one
crisp fall day
she came by my house
she poured herself
a tall glass of vodka
neat, no ice
our usual discussion
our almost grown children
our men, here and gone
our poetry, prizes, invitations
still sisters in that way.

We were inseparable
before I bought the farm
in New Hampshire
her move to a big house
no longer married, not
neighbors, young mothers
sharing silk dresses, wool coats
leather purses and high heels
our kids in the pool
our husbands at the grill
we mated our Dalmatians
for eight polka-dot pups
suburban women on the cusp
of having it all.

We'd made it, Anne and I
through many laps, relapses
I kept her alive
she gave me the courage
to become the writer
I was afraid to be.

We'd felt the distance
with our separations
her mood blacker
her mind foggier

writing like a fugitive
running, running
keeping one length ahead
of an invisible enemy
scaring me
reminding me
of Plath penning *Ariel*
before laying her head
inside the gas stove.

In the burnt orange afternoon
like so many others
we went over Anne's proofs
ate thick tuna sandwiches
and when she left me
she promised me
she wasn't John Berryman
our confessional brother
another suicidal poet
too recently gone.

She'd reached out before
after popping too many
of her kill-me pills
woozy and pale, she'd said:
*You won't get another chance
to save me.*

I knew she was done
I knew but believed her:
not that day, not that one
the leaves butter yellow
the sky Prussian blue
when she drove off
in her old red Cougar
I waved goodbye
but I meant see you soon.

Charles Bukowski
(1920-1994)

Bukowski's Barfly Lover
(Jane Cooney Baker)

He was the dirty old man
of American letters
proud of his boozing
womanizing
down 'n' out
ugly ways
but when I met him
a virgin a decade
younger than I was
in an alcoholic daze while
strangers paid for my drinks
and maybe, sometimes
we went out in the alley too.

Hank was the anti-hero
his maverick art forged
from the daily grind
in coarse language
working class pain
rooming house blues
but when I met him
he was unpublished
struggling to keep a job
struggling to pay the rent
in filthy flophouses
in the red light district.

The hardcore bard
of the LA demimonde
peeling back the sheen
to show the sickly underside
but when I met him
he thought he had something
he did
he had trouble
he had drama
he had a drinking partner
he had a drinking problem
he had woman troubles
to deal with
and write about
for the rest of his life.

Bukowski's First Wife
(Barbara Frye)

I was born misshapen, afraid
no man would ever marry me
but Hank promised to
before we even met
he was so grateful
I recognized his genius
I published his work
in my little magazine
I was so grateful
I moved to LA
shocking him
with my odd build.

But God bless him
he took me
to bed
then to Vegas
like he'd promised.

My wealthy Texas family
co-founded an airline
but I said we'd make it
on our own
and live in a house
in a decent neighborhood
while I published his poems
and he supported us.

I was so grateful
for our two years together
until I lost our baby
until I found a lover
and left him flat.

He said I knew
what I wanted
and it wasn't him—
said he knew
more women like me
than any other kind.

The Mother of His Child
(Frances Smith)

East Hollywood rundown motor courts
brassy cocktail lounges, cracked asphalt
ultra-wide boulevards and Ned's
Liquor Store a quick walk away
from where I found him
on the bum, living small
in a seedy boardinghouse
kitchenette, murphy bed
big roaches and strict rules
about typing poems at night.

His parents' deaths aroused
no sorrow, raised cash
he was careful then
with money after Jane
passed from cirrhosis
her yellow robe a shroud
hanging in his closet
in the deep blue low
he hid the razors
the knives and scissors
his poems in gritty chapbooks
street stories in a collection
of the raw realities
of poverty, heartbreak.

He called me one night late
drunk and demanding
I go to him
I went to him
by bus and cab
we talked until morning
I loved him, so big
soft, tender, gorgeous
and that's why I stayed.

There is always one woman
to save you from another
and as she saves you
she makes ready

to destroy you
is what he thought, said
I saved him.

But I was 42
and pregnant
with Marina Louise
so we moved to a bungalow
he worked the graveyard shift
a devoted loving father
even after
the morning he came home
told me to move out
because he knew
I was unhappy
with his drinking
with his hours
with him

and that's why I left him.

The Poet's Young Lover
(Linda King)

I brought it to him
and he knew
one day
I would take it away.

He was the victim
of his first love
he believed all women
were women like Jane
whores who slept around
he was the victim
of a father who beat him
for his acne, dyslexia
he was the victim
of poverty, an outsider
he built up a grudge
he took with him
for the rest of his days.

I thought he was ugly
too old too fat too scruffy
but I sketched him and
he made me laugh
he made me feel
alive while I sculpted
his head I fell in love
with his voice, his mind.

I showed him
how to drink less
how to eat cold plums in bed
grow his hair long, a beard
hip clothes, floral shirts
bell bottom jeans I taught him
how to love a woman.

Never envy a man
his lady he said
behind it lies
a living hell but
he was hell too.

He cheated on me
a rich bitch in the Hills
when he left her for me
she vomited her false teeth
I tracked him to another
chick's place and chucked
a full beer through her
bay window, took him
home with me.

His love for me
drove him mad
the old rage inside
punched me in the face
over and over
we broke up
and he returned
the sculpted head
and we made up
I brought it back.

We fought, he shot
himself
in the leg, drunk
arrested but so famous
the cops gave him coffee
let him call me to make up.

After I miscarried
I stole his typewriter
his first edition books
his original drawings
and one day I took
the sculpted head
and that
was that

he was no longer
in my blood.

The Poet's Last Wife
(Linda Lee Beighle)

He said he didn't know
how many bottles of beer
he consumed
while waiting for things
to get better.

Never a mainstream writer
never a sellout, always direct
too honest and offensive
the bard of the barroom
he didn't see himself
as an alcoholic, said
he could quit drinking
at any time
for any reason—
but didn't.

His work was powerful
little atomic bombs
that went off in your hands—
his life did too.
So much life
all over the place!

He had a direct style
touched with humor
an original voice
a famous weekly column
sex stories he invented
because he had none
before Linda King
he had little
after I came along
the mailman asked him
how he got all the young chicks
and he said the problem was
how to get rid of them.

I was one of them, then
I got rid of them.

The Poet's Widow
(Linda Lee Bukowski)

I ran the Dew Drop Inn
health food restaurant
I followed guru rules:
no sex
on the road to enlightenment
and he liked that
tired of performing
with me he could just be
kick back, dream
of being famous—
not to be confused
with ambition he liked
doing nothing, drinking
lounging in his boxers.

He'd spent most of his time
in the bowels of the PO
or at the race track
or drinking diet Schlitz
in his shit-brown apartment
with coffee cans of grease
one 40-watt bulb, a hovel
full of empties and trash.

His popularity in Germany
France, all over Europe
popped when he punked
drunk and nasty, abusive
to journalists and the media
and we laughed
and the people loved it
and the royalties poured in
and we bought a nice house
in San Pedro with roses
a wide green lawn
sweet guava trees
under his private office
a balcony he sat out on
each night with a bottle
of good French wine.

Once when we split up
I stopped eating
and he got scared enough
to marry me, Hank
dressed in a cream suit
snake skin shoes, happier
than I'd ever seen him.

Hollywood came calling
for screenplays and his life
story, a documentary
filmed at our house
and he kicked me
took a swing
called me terrible names—
not a good look
but direct, honest
and funny, I thought.

At the peak of his fame
he crashed hard
withering, all bones
quit drinking
kept writing
kept me laughing
'til the very end.

Prose Biographies

The descendant of an elite Boston Brahmin family, Thomas Stearns Eliot (**T.S. Eliot**) was born in St. Louis and attended Harvard, the Sorbonne, and Oxford. He lived in London and worked as a teacher, a banker, and an editor at Faber and Faber. In 1927, he renounced his American citizenship and became a British citizen.

Eliot married Vivienne Haigh-Wood in 1915, but their marriage was unhappy. They separated in 1933. She suffered from multiple physical ailments and was committed by her brother to an asylum in 1938, where she remained until her death in 1947. Eliot never visited her during that time.

In love with Emily Hale since his Harvard undergrad days, Eliot wooed her from 1933 to 1946, mostly via letters. However, he refused to marry her. She donated his love letters to the Princeton University Library with directions not to unseal them until fifty years after their deaths (which was in 2020).

Eliot befriended Mary Trevelyan in 1938, and they remained companions for almost twenty years. He turned down her multiple offers of marriage. In 1957 he shocked her by marrying 30-year-old Esmé Valerie Fletcher, his devoted secretary at Faber since 1949.

After a brief but happy marriage, Eliot died. His widow devoted herself to his legacy until her own death in 2012.

Eliot's poetry was unusual and exciting, and he influenced other important writers including James Joyce, F. Scott Fitzgerald, and Bob Dylan. Considered one of the major poets of the 20th century, he was awarded the Nobel Prize for Literature in 1948.

One of the 20th century's greatest poets, **Ted Hughes** was born Edward James Hughes in Yorkshire on the moorland. After attending Cambridge University, he worked odd jobs until meeting American poet and Fulbright scholar Sylvia Plath, who helped him launch his career.

His marriage to Plath was fulfilling and productive as the two poets encouraged each other to expand their individual voices. Hughes' work focused on the beauty and savage violence of nature. He employed alternative means for reaching subconscious thought and imagery including the use of tarot, astrology, and the Ouija board.

The couple moved to the countryside to raise their two children. But after she discovered he was having an affair with the woman subletting their London flat, Plath separated from Hughes. She moved to London with their children, where she wrote the poems that made her name before taking her own life. Hughes became her literary executor, publishing her poetry, and she became an international sensation.

Hughes' mistress Assia Wevill died by suicide, also by gas stove asphyxiation. She killed their 4-year-old daughter as well.

In 1970, Hughes married neighbor Carol Orchard. They remained together despite his myriad affairs.

His work was critically acclaimed and widely read. He was appointed Poet Laureate of England, a post he held from 1984 until his death.

A rock star poet in the 1920s, **Edna St. Vincent Millay** was the first woman to win the Pulitzer Prize for Poetry. She led an unconventional life and was highly regarded for her literary genius. Her work touched on women's sexuality, the politics of war, and other social issues. Her public readings were wildly popular, her stage presence flamboyant and exciting.

Millay grew up in Maine. Her independent mother divorced her father, working as a traveling nurse and leaving young Vincent in charge of her two sisters.

A wealthy patron noted the 20-year-old's writing talent and paid for Vincent to attend Vassar College. After graduating, she moved to the budding bohemia of Greenwich Village. She had sexual relationships with both men and women.

After a long illness triggered by her mother's herbal abortion remedy, Millay married the man she'd hired to nurse her. A wealthy 42-year-old Dutch merchant, Eugen Jan Boissevain was the widower of an American suffragist and a self-proclaimed feminist. The couple lived on an old blueberry farm in the Berkshires they called Steepletop, and on Ragged Island in Casco Bay, Maine.

Eugen managed Millay's literary career and the domestic duties, ferrying her to her speaking engagements. They were proponents of free love and had an open marriage. Her lovers included the young college student George Dillon.

After she fell out of a moving vehicle, Millay became addicted to morphine. Eugen died in 1949; a year later Millay took a fatal spill on the stairs. They are buried together at Steepletop, now an artists' residency and historic landmark.

You might recognize these lines from Millay's famous poem "The Fig":

My candle burns at both ends;
It will not last the night;
But oh, my foes, and oh, my friends—
It gives a lovely light!

Welsh poet and author of "Do not go gentle into that good night," **Dylan Thomas** became internationally famous in his lifetime, partly due to his reputation as what he called "a drunken and doomed poet." He was also a hardworking writer, a masterful performer, and one of the most influential poets of his generation.

Born in the seaside city of Swansea to an English teacher father and a coddling mother, Dylan suffered from asthma. He left school at 16 to work as a journalist, and spent time acting in and producing plays. He wrote poetry and became a heavy drinker.

In 1936, Thomas met Caitlin Macnamara at a London pub. Drinking companions, the two married the following year. He wrote scripts for the BBC and films for the British government.

The couple settled in Laugharne, Wales, to raise their three children. A home was purchased for them by one of Dylan's patrons; called the Boat House, it included a separate writing shed overlooking an estuary he nicknamed "the bronchial heronry." He also rented a house across from the town pub for his aging parents. He was often unwell, and money was always scarce.

Thomas made four trips to America in the early 1950s, where he was famous for his powerful readings and wild carousing. On the first tour, he read at forty different venues around the country; on the second tour, he read at forty-six. On the third visit he developed gout and gastritis, and broke his arm in a fall. When he returned home, he was experiencing blackouts and had a racking cough. His fourth and final visit to the US came during a bad smog event in New York. When he developed bronchitis and possibly pneumonia, a doctor provided shots of cortisone and morphine.

By the time Thomas arrived at a hospital emergency room, he was in a coma. When his wife saw him near death, she became violent and was committed to an asylum. She brought Dylan's body home by ship to be buried in the village of Laugharne.

Dylan Thomas is still famous, his unique voice and obtuse verse beloved by modern readers. The Boat House is now a museum, and there is a statue of the poet in Swansea.

Robert Traill Spence Lowell IV (**Robert Lowell**) was born into an elite Boston Brahmin family. His father was a Navy commander, his mother a descendent of *Mayflower* passengers. Amy Lowell, a famous poet, was his cousin, and the poet James Russell Lowell was his great-grand uncle. He wrote poetry about his home city and his ancestors.

Nicknamed Cal, Lowell was a bully in boarding school and a dropout at Harvard. While still in college, he had a fistfight with his father over his parents' rejection of his girlfriend Anne Dick. He ran away to Nashville, pitching a tent on the lawn of poet Alan Tate. Lowell then attended Kenyon College, where Tate taught poetry. After graduating with honors, Lowell taught at a number of universities—including Harvard.

In 1940, Lowell married novelist Jean Stafford. Their unhappy marriage ended in 1948, and the following year he married writer Elizabeth Hardwick. They had a daughter, and their marriage lasted more than twenty years. She forgave his affairs and tended to him during his mental breakdowns. Lowell suffered from bipolar disorder, often falling in love while manic, crashing and institutionalized when depressed.

He left Hardwick in 1970 for Guinness heir and writer Caroline Blackwood, with whom he had a son. They lived on a Guinness family estate in England, then on one in Ireland. Their marriage was rocky due to their alcohol abuse.

At age 60, Lowell suffered a fatal heart attack. He was in a taxi on the way to Hardwick's home in New York.

Lowell called his work "verse autobiography."

Two of his poetry books won the Pulitzer Prize. His contribution to the confessional poetry movement was significant. Anne Sexton and Sylvia Plath were inspired by his work; he taught both poets in his classes at Boston University.

Elizabeth Bishop had a difficult childhood due to ill health and the absence of her parents. Her father had left them, and her mother suffered from mental illness; she was institutionalized when Bishop was a child.

She was raised by relatives in Nova Scotia and Massachusetts. Often bedridden due to respiratory illnesses, she was an a avid reader. She began writing poetry at age 8.

After college, Bishop traveled. She focused on poetry, writing slowly and rewriting her work many times over.

Bishop lived in a variety of inspirational settings including Key West, Rio de Janeiro, Seattle, Boston, and coastal Maine. She loved being in nature, fishing, hiking, and exploring the flora and fauna she would incorporate into her poems.

A perfectionist, she spent years polishing the 101 highly acclaimed poems published in her lifetime. She steadfastly refused to be featured in women-only anthologies; she wanted to be judged only on her work, not her gender—as the male writers were.

Bishop believed her sexual passions had to be hidden. She used alcohol in order to deal with her emotions and find the courage to pursue her life's choices. She referred to her female lovers as "friends" and indulged in drinking bouts that affected her health.

Bishop died in Boston in her condo overlooking the harbor. She is considered one of the most important 20th century American poets.

An American writer of poetry, drama, essays, and music criticism, **LeRoi Jones** produced multiple works on the history of African-American culture. His themes ranged from black liberation to jazz and blues history to extremist politics. He won literary awards but earned widespread criticism for his expressions of racism, misogyny, homophobia, anti-Semitism, and the promotion of violence.

Jones was born and raised in Newark, New Jersey,

in a working class family. After attending Rutgers, Jones transferred to Howard University, but eventually dropped out. He enlisted in the US Air Force and was stationed in Puerto Rico. While there, he began reading Beat poetry and writing poems.

He moved to Greenwich Village and worked for a record magazine, marrying his Jewish coworker, Hettie Cohen; the couple had two daughters. Together they founded a small press and a literary magazine in order to publish Beat poets like Allen Ginsburg and Jack Kerouac. Jones had an affair with the white beat poet Diane DiPrima, which resulted in another daughter.

His first poetry collection was published in 1961, and his book on the history of jazz and blues in America was released in 1963. *Dutchman*, in which a white woman accosts a black man on the subway, won an Obie for Best American Play in 1964.

Leaving his wife and children on the Lower East Side, Jones moved to Harlem and created the Black Arts Reparatory/Theater School, launching a nationwide surge in black arts. When a charge of improper use of federal funds closed the theater, he returned to Newark. He married Sylvia Robinson, an actress and Newark community organizer.

After meeting the leader of the Islamic Kawaida movement that prescribed the adoption of African names and customs, Jones changed his name to Amiri Baraka, his wife's to Amina Baraka. They raised five children and founded Spirit House, a theater and artists' residence.

He eventually distanced himself from the black nationalism movement in favor of Marxism and third-world liberation. He taught at several colleges in the African-American studies departments, and was nominated the Poet Laureate of New Jersey. But he was asked to leave the post in 2002 after a public reading of his poem "Somebody Blew Up America" (which includes anti-Semitic content). When he refused to quit the post, the governor abolished the position.

Jones was an important literary influence as co-founder of the Black Arts Movement, which helped open the door to publishing for black writers.

Anne Sexton was born Anne Gray Harvey in Newton, Massachusetts. After high school she worked for a modeling agency in Boston. She eloped with Alfred Muller Sexton II while engaged to another man. The couple lived in Newton and had two daughters. The marriage lasted for decades despite her affairs and his violent temper.

She began having manic episodes in 1954, and underwent years of therapy with Dr. Martin Orne. After he encouraged her to write, she began composing formal poetry. At his suggestion, she attended classes including a poetry workshop at the Boston Center for Adult Education. There she met Maxine Kumin, a Newton neighbor. The two women became close friends and critiqued each other's work for decades.

Sexton audited a class at Boston University taught by Robert Lowell, where she met Sylvia Plath and George Starbuck; the three writers would go to the Ritz Hotel after class and drink martinis. Starbuck recalled the two women discussing their suicide attempts. He was the editor for her first poetry book, and her paramour. Her book *Live or Die* won the Pulitzer Prize for Poetry in 1967.

After Starbuck, Sexton had multiple affairs, finally divorcing in 1973. By that time she was involved in an affair with her latest therapist.

On her final day of life, she visited Kumin for lunch before sitting in a garaged car with the engine running.

Anne Sexton wrote confessional poetry about her suicidal thoughts, her bipolar disorder, and the intimate details of her life. Even though she never attended college, she was given a fellowship at Radcliffe, received honorary degrees, and was the recipient of many grants, prizes, and accolades. She broke barriers, writing about prohibited subjects ranging from her own stints in mental hospitals to incest, abortion, menopause, and sex. The controversy over her chosen topics also made her popular with the general public, including people who normally did not read poetry. Her live readings were always packed because of her engaging stage presence. She also performed her work to music with the jazz-rock group Her Kind.

Musicians who have cited Sexton's work as an influence include Madonna, Morrissey, and Peter Gabriel. Many poets and writers have been inspired by her unique voice, her careful craft, her bravery and honesty.

An underground writer of immense popularity, **Charles Bukowski** documented lowlife Los Angeles: the poverty, the flophouses, the hookers and street hustlers, the lousy pay for demeaning jobs, the debilitated alcoholics. He published in small literary magazines for over fifty years, and more than sixty books of his poetry, fiction, and essays have been released.

Born in Germany to an American father and a German mother, Chuck moved with his family to Baltimore in 1923, then to Los Angeles in 1930. His father was abusive, and Chuck was teased for his accent, acne, and unhip clothes. Rage built up and he began using alcohol to deal with the pain of his living situation.

After graduating from Los Angeles High School and spending two years at Los Angeles City College, he moved to New York and began working odd jobs so he could write. His lack of success discouraged him, however, and he quit writing for a decade. During that time, he fell in love with Jane Cooney Baker, a severe alcoholic. He recounted this period of his life in his later work using an alter-ego named Henry Chinaski, and he penned the screenplay for the movie version; *Barfly* starred Mickey Rourke as Chinaski and Faye Dunaway as Jane.

In 1955, Bukowski married the Texas magazine publisher Barbara Frye. He worked as a clerk at the post office. The couple were divorced in 1958. While living with girlfriend Frances Smith and their daughter Marina, he began writing "Notes of a Dirty Old Man" for the underground newspaper *Open City*. His column was picked up by the *Los Angeles Free Press*. The oddball, funny, seamy column made his name.

Bukowski published his first book with the tiny Black Sparrow Press. His public poetry readings were drunken brawls, the audience heckling and the drunk poet yelling back. These unruly events established his reputation as a wildly unpredictable and entertaining performer. His popularity turned Black Sparrow into a successful business and he remained loyal, publishing his books with them for the rest of his life.

Bukowski had multiple affairs with young women, eventually marrying Linda Lee Beighle, the owner of a health food store. They lived in a nice home in San Pedro until he died from leukemia at age 73.

Criticized by some for his sexism and rowdy alcoholism, Bukowski was a controversial literary figure. However, he has served as an inspiration to many poets, musicians, and writers. His work is entertaining for those with the appropriate sensibility.

References

Matthew Hollis, *The Waste Land: A Biography of a Poem*, W.W. Norton, 2022.

Lyndall Gordon, *The Hyacinth Girl: T.S. Eliot's Hidden Muse*, W.W. Norton, 2022.

Christopher Reid, *Letters of Ted Hughes*, Farrar, Straus and Giroux, 2007.

Jonathan Bate, *Ted Hughes: The Unauthorized Life*, Harper, 2015.

Daniel Mark Epstein, *What Lips My Lips Have Kissed: The Loves and Love Poems of Edna St. Vincent Millay*, Henry Holt and Company, 2001.

Caitlin Thomas, *My Life with Dylan Thomas*, Henry Holt and Company, 1986.

Andrew Lycett, *Dylan Thomas: A New Life*, Overlook Press, 2004.

John Brinnin, *Dylan Thomas in America*, Viking, 1957.

Robert Lowell, *Memoirs*, Farrar, Straus and Giroux, 2022.

Jeffrey Meyers, *Robert Lowell in Love*, University of Massachusetts Press, 2015.

Nancy Schoenberger, *Dangerous Muse: The Life of Lady Caroline Blackwood*, DaCapo Press, 2002.

Megan Marshall, *Elizabeth Bishop: A Miracle at Breakfast*, Mariner Books, 2017.

Michael Sledge, *The More I Owe You*, Counterpoint, 2010.

Amiri Baraka, *The Autobiography of LeRoi Jones*, Lawrence Hill Press, 1997.

Hettie Jones, *How I Became Hettie Jones*, Grove Press, 1996.

Diane Middlebrook, *Anne Sexton: A Biography*, Vintage, 1992.

Howard Sounes, *Charles Bukowski: Locked in the Arms of a Crazy Life*, Grove Press, 1998.

Maggie Doherty, *The Equivalents: A Story of Art, Female Friendship, and Liberation in the 1960s*, Vintage, 2021.

Suggested Reading

T.S. Eliot:
The Wasteland and Other Poems
The Four Quartets: A Poem

Ted Hughes:
The Hawk in the Rain: Poems
Crow
Iron Man
Birthday Letters: Poems

Edna St. Vincent Millay:
A Few Figs from Thistles
"Renascence"

Dylan Thomas:
Portrait of the Artist as a Young Dog
A Child's Christmas in Wales
Under Milk Wood

Robert Lowell:
Life Studies
For the Union Dead
Lord Weary's Castle

Elizabeth Bishop:
North & South
A Cold Spring
Questions of Travel
Geography III

LeRoi Jones:
Blues People
Preface to a Twenty Volume Suicide Note
Dutchman
"Somebody Blew Up America"

Anne Sexton:
All My Pretty Ones
Live or Die: Poems
The Death Notebooks
Transformations

Charles Bukowski:
Factotum
Ham on Rye: A Novel
Love is a Dog from Hell

Acknowledgments

My deepest gratitude for essential feedback and moral support goes to fellow writers Alan, Tim, Maxine, Mike, Leah, Benita, Diane, and Joe. Extra special thanks to James, and to my proofreader Mel.

I must also express my thanks to the following publications for including some of these poems, sometimes in altered form, sometimes under another (pen) name, in their pages:

Misfit Magazine:
The Poet's Muse (Emily Hale), The Poet's Widow (Carol Orchard Hughes), The Poet's Wife (Caitlin Macnamara Thomas), The Poet's First Wife (Jean Stafford), The Poet's Ex (Hettie Cohen Jones), The Poet's Widow (Amina Baraka)

Main Street Rag:
The Poet's First Wife (Sylvia Plath), The Poet's Lover (Assia Wevill), The Poet's Second Wife (Carol Orchard Hughes)

Prachya Review:
The Poet's First Wife (Vivienne Haigh-Wood Eliot), The Poet's Poet Wife (Sylvia Plath)

Synchronized Chaos:
Elizabeth Bishop on Her Friends, Elizabeth Bishop on Her Thirst

Lowestoft Chronicle:
The Poet's Lota (as "Elizabeth Bishop in Brazil")

Poetry Superhighway:
The Poet's Widow (Linda Lee Bukowski)

The Poetry Cove:
Bukowski's Barfly Lover (Jane Cooney Baker)

Virginia Aronson is the author of many published books, both nonfiction and fiction. Her poems have appeared in literary journals and in books from small poetry presses. *Itako* was published by Clare Songbirds Publishing House in 2020. Originally from Boston, she currently resides in the lush and lurid tropics, where she works as the director for a food and nutrition foundation.